Contents

21st Century – page 2
Transfers I – page 5
First Goals I – page 8
Red Cards – page 10
Memorable Goals – page 13
Memorable Games – page 16
Transfers II – page 18
Cup Games – page 21
First Goals II – page 23
European Games – page 25

21st Century answers – page 29
Transfers I answers – page 33
First Goals I answers – page 37
Red Cards answers – page 39
Memorable Goals answers – page 42
Memorable Games answers – page 45
Transfers II answers – page 48
Cup Games answers – page 52
First Goals II answers – page 55
European Games answers – page 57

21st Century

1) In what year did Ashley Cole move from Arsenal to Chelsea?

2) In which season did the Arsenal 'Invincibles' go unbeaten for the whole league season?

3) In what year did club servant Pat Rice retire from his role as Assistant Manager?

4) Who did Arsenal play in Mikel Arteta's first game as manager, and what was the score?

5) Aaron Ramsey suffered an horrendous leg break after a challenge from which Stoke player in 2010?

6) Which Birmingham City player was responsible for the tackle that broke Eduardo's leg in 2008?

7) Which two Arsenal players scored hat-tricks in the 6-1 win over Southampton in 2003?

8) Who became the first Costa Rican player to represent Arsenal in the Premier League when he debuted in 2014?

9) How old was Jens Lehmann when he made his final appearance for the club against Blackpool in April 2011?

10) Theo Walcott scored his first Premier League hat-trick against which team in August 2010?

11) Arsenal won 2-1 away to Manchester City in August 2003 despite a comical own goal from which player?

12) Thierry Henry surpassed Ian Wright as Arsenal's leading scorer of all time when he scored his 186th goal for the club against which European club?

13) Which team ended Arsenal's unbeaten run of 49 games in October 2004?

14) Arsenal won 4-2 in their final ever match at Highbury against which opponent?

15) Arsenal drew 1-1 against Aston Villa in their first game at the Emirates Stadium, which Villa scored the first Premier League goal at the ground?

16) Who did Arsenal beat 1-0 away from home in Arsene Wenger's last game in charge?

Transfers I

1) Lauren arrived from which Spanish club in May 2000?

2) Club stalwart Nigel Winterburn left Arsenal in the summer of 2000 to join which team?

3) Which midfielder was signed from Marseille in July 2000?

4) Which young English forward was bought from Everton in 2001?

5) Which two players left the club to join Barcelona in July 2000?

6) From where did Arsenal sign Giovanni van Bronckhorst in 2001?

7) Which future England international defender was sold to Birmingham in 2003?

8) Where did legendary goalkeeper David Seaman go after leaving Arsenal?

9) From which German club did Arsenal sign Jens Lehmann?

10) Robin van Persie was bought from which team in 2004?

11) Which central midfielder was signed on a free from Marseille in July 2004?

12) Who did Martin Keown sign for after leaving Arsenal in 2004?

13) Which striker was bought from FC Copenhagen in 2005?

14) Patrick Viera was sold to which Italian club in 2005?

15) From which Premier League rival did Arsenal buy William Gallas in 2006?

16) Sol Campbell went to which team after being released in 2006?

17) Which young midfielder was signed from Cardiff in the summer of 2008?

18) To which English club did Arsenal sell Freddie Ljungberg in 2007?

19) Which Spanish club bought Aleksandr Hleb from Arsenal in 2008?

20) Which defender arrived from Ajax in July 2009?

21) Which two players were sold to Manchester City in July 2009?

First Goals I – Name the clubs that these players scored their first goal for Arsenal against

1) Robert Pires

2) Alexandre Lacazette

3) Pierre-Emerick Aubameyang

4) Sylvain Wiltord

5) Robin Van Persie

6) Gilberto Silva

7) Jose Antonio Reyes

8) Theo Walcott

9) Ashley Cole

10) Bacary Sagna

11) Aaron Ramsey

12) Jack Wilshere

13) Samir Nasri

14) Andrey Arshavin

Red Cards

1) Who was sent off on his Premier League debut against Newcastle in August 2011?

2) Alex Oxlade-Chamberlain handled the ball on the line versus Chelsea in 2014, but which player was incorrectly sent off instead?

3) Robin van Persie was given a second yellow card against Barcelona in March 2011 for what contentious reason?

4) Ray Parlour was controversially sent off against which team in December 2001?

5) Sol Campbell was sent off for an alleged elbow on which Manchester United player in April 2003?

6) Arsenal claimed a 1-1 draw with Middlesbrough despite being down to ten men after which defender saw red in February 2007?

7) Patrick Vieira was sent off after a clash with which Leicester City player in August 2001?

8) Who was dismissed during the game with Southampton in April 2018?

9) Which player was dismissed in the 4-4 draw with Newcastle in 2011?

10) Laurent Koscielny was sent off early in the first half against which side during the last game of the 2017 season?

11) Which two Arsenal players were sent off versus Chelsea in September 2015?

12) Arsenal claimed a 1-1 draw away to which side in the Champions League in November 2004 despite both Lauren and Patrick Vieira seeing red?

13) Which striker was sent off in the away fixture with Crystal Palace in January 2020?

14) Which defender was dismissed in the 2-2 draw with Chelsea in January 2020?

15) Wojciech Szczesny was sent off in the first half of a 2-0 loss to which club in the last 16 Champions League tie in February 2014?

Memorable Goals

1) Who did Thierry Henry score his final goal for Arsenal against?

2) Thierry Henry returned to Arsenal in 2012 and scored on his second debut against which team in the FA Cup?

3) How many times did Andrey Arshavin score against Liverpool in the April 2009 meeting between the two sides?

4) Robert Pires produced a sublime lob against Aston Villa in 2002, which goalkeeper did he score past?

5) Which player became Arsenal's youngest ever goal scorer by netting in the League Cup versus Wolves aged 16 years 6 months 28 days in December 2003?

6) Which team did Dennis Bergkamp score his final goal against in 2006?

7) Bergkamp scored the Premier League goal of the season after produced a magnificent turn on which Newcastle defender in March 2002?

8) Thierry Henry scored his incredible solo goal against Spurs in November 2002 past which goalkeeper?

9) Which player scored the Premier League goal of the season for 2013/14 and 2014/15?

10) Which full back won the goal of the month competition twice in the year 2000 for goals against Sheffield Wednesday and Chelsea?

11) Patrick Vieira produced a wonderful chipped finish against which team in May 2005?

12) Aaron Ramsey scored the November 2013 goal of the month with his strike from the edge of the box versus which team?

13) Olivier Giroud scored with a spectacular scorpion flick against which team in January 2017?

14) Aaron Ramsey finished off a wonderful team goal away to which London club in October 2018?

Memorable Games

1) Which former Arsenal player was sent off in the 5-2 win over Spurs in November 2012?

2) Who scored a late brace as the Gunners won 5-2 against Tottenham in February 2012?

3) Arsenal won the league at White Hart Lane in April 2004, what was the score that day?

4) Arsenal threw away a four-goal lead to draw 4-4 with Newcastle in 2011, but which player had opened the scoring in the first minute?

5) Arsenal were pegged back to a 4-4 draw with Spurs in October 2008 after which player scored an injury-time equaliser?

6) Which two Arsenal players scored during their humiliating 8-2 defeat against Manchester United in 2011?

7) Who scored the final goal as Arsenal destroyed Middlesbrough 7-0 in January 2006?

8) What was the final score as Arsenal tore Everton apart in May 2005?

9) Arsenal faced Chelsea in Arsene Wenger's 1000th game as manager, what was the score?

10) Arsenal beat Tottenham 5-4 away from home in November 2004, which Arsenal player scored from the penalty spot?

11) Who did Arsenal beat 4-3 on the opening day of the 2017/18 Premier League season?

12) Who scored a hat-trick as Arsenal won 5-1 at West ham 5-1 in December 2016?

Transfers II

1) Arsenal signed which central midfielder from Everton in 2011?

2) From which German side did Arsenal sign Per Mertesacker?

3) Olivier Giroud was bought from which French side in 2012?

4) From which Spanish club did Arsenal buy Santi Cazorla in 2012?

5) Who returned to the club from AC Milan in 2013?

6) Lukasz Fabianski signed for which team after leaving Arsenal in 2014?

7) Which Newcastle defender did Arsenal buy in 2014?

8) Who did Arsenal buy from Borussia Mönchengladbach in 2016?

9) Lukas Podolski was sold to who in 2015?

10) From which English club was Rob Holding bought in 2016?

11) Shkodran Mustafi was bought from which Spanish club in 2016?

12) Which attacking player was sold to Werder Bremen in August 2016?

13) Alexandre Lacazette was bought from which team in 2017?

14) Who did Arsenal buy from Bayer Leverkusen in June 2018?

15) Which defender was sold to West Brom in 2017?

16) Which midfielder was sold to Liverpool in August 2017?

17) Which experienced defender signed on a free from Juventus in 2018?

18) Jack Wilshere left the club in 2018 to sign for which club on a free?

19) Which attacker was bought from Lille in the summer of 2019?

20) Arsenal bought which defender from Celtic in 2019?

21) Which attacker was sold to Everton in August 2019?

Cup Games

1) How many FA Cup winner's medals did Aaron Ramsey collect during his time at Arsenal?

2) Arsenal beat Southampton 1-0 in the 2003 FA Cup final, who scored the winner?

3) Arsenal beat Hull City 3-2 after extra time in the 2014 FA Cup final, who scored the equaliser in normal time for the Gunners?

4) Arsenal beat Liverpool 6-3 away from home in the League Cup Quarter Final of 2007, who scored four times for the Gunners?

5) Who scored the opening goal in the 2017 FA Cup final win over Chelsea?

6) Which team did Arsenal beat 4-0 in the 2015 FA Cup final?

7) Who scored the decisive spot kick as Arsenal beat Manchester United on penalties in the 2005 FA Cup final?

8) Nottingham Forest knocked Arsenal out of the FA Cup at the 3rd round stage in 2018 by what score-line?

9) Who scored the last-minute winner for Birmingham to clinch the League Cup in 2011?

10) Arsenal lost to Middlesbrough in the 2004 League Cup Semi Final, who was in goal for Arsenal in the 2nd leg?

11) Who scored twice for Chelsea as they defeated Arsenal 2-1 in the 2007 League Cup Final?

12) Liverpool and Arsenal played out an unbelievable tie in the League Cup in October 2019, what was the score in normal time before Liverpool won on penalties?

First Goals II

1) Sol Campbell

2) Cesc Fàbregas

3) Alex Oxlade-Chamberlain

4) Per Mertesacker

5) Lukas Podolski

6) Olivier Giroud

7) Santi Cazorla

8) Nicklas Bendtner

9) Hector Bellerín

10) Alexis Sanchez

11) Mesut Özil

12) Danny Welbeck

13) Granit Xhaka

14) Nicolas Pepe

European Games

1) Thierry Henry scored a stunning solo goal against Real Madrid in 2006, which goalkeeper did he score past?

2) Arsenal recorded a famous away win by demolishing Inter Milan in the Champions League in November 2003, what was the final score?

3) Who scored the late winner as Chelsea knocked Arsenal out of the Champions League at the Quarter Final stage in 2004?

4) Who scored the only goal of the tie as Arsenal reached the 2006 Champions League Final by beating Villarreal on aggregate?

5) Jens Lehmann made a vital, late penalty save from which player to prevent that 2006 Semi Final from going to extra time?

6) Who scored the opening goal in the 2006 Champions League Final?

7) Which English team knocked Arsenal out of the 2008 Champions League in the Quarter Finals?

8) Which team knocked Arsenal out of the Champions League at the last 16 stage in both 2013 and 2014?

9) Which side did Arsenal knock out of Champions League in the qualifying round in 2009?

10) Arsenal lost to Atletico Madrid in the 2018 Europa League Semi Final, who scored the only goal in the 1-0 defeat in the 2nd leg?

11) Who scored the Arsenal goal as they lost 4-1 in the 2019 Europa League Final against Chelsea?

12) Arsenal lost the 2000 UEFA Cup Final 4-1 on penalties to which team?

13) Who scored the late winner as Arsenal beat Barcelona 2-1 in the 1st leg of their Champions League knockout tie in 2011?

14) Which team did Arsenal beat 7-0 in the Champions League in October 2007?

21st Century – Answers

1) In what year did Ashley Cole move from Arsenal to Chelsea?
2006

2) In which season did the Arsenal 'Invincibles' go unbeaten for the whole league season?
2003/04

3) In what year did club servant Pat Rice retire from his role as Assistant Manager?
2012

4) Who did Arsenal play in Mikel Arteta's first game as manager, and what was the score?
Bournemouth 1-1 Arsenal

5) Aaron Ramsey suffered an horrendous leg break after a challenge from which Stoke player in 2010?
Ryan Shawcross

6) Which Birmingham City player was responsible for the tackle that broke Eduardo's leg in 2008?
Martin Taylor

7) Which two Arsenal players scored hat-tricks in the 6-1 win over Southampton in 2003?
Robert Pires and Jermaine Pennant

8) Who became the first Costa Rican player to represent Arsenal in the Premier League when he debuted in 2014?
Joel Campbell

9) How old was Jens Lehmann when he made his final appearance for the club against Blackpool in April 2011?
41

10) Theo Walcott scored his first Premier League hat-trick against which team in August 2010?
Blackpool

11) Arsenal won 2-1 away to Manchester City in August 2003 despite a comical own goal from which player?
Lauren

12) Thierry Henry surpassed Ian Wright as Arsenal's leading scorer of all time when he scored his 186th goal for the club against which European club?
Sparta Prague

13) Which team ended Arsenal's unbeaten run of 49 games in October 2004?
Manchester United

14) Arsenal won 4-2 in their final ever match at Highbury against which opponent?
Wigan Athletic

15) Arsenal drew 1-1 against Aston Villa in their first game at the Emirates Stadium, which Villa scored the first Premier League goal at the ground?
Olof Mellberg

16) Who did Arsenal beat 1-0 away from home in Arsene Wenger's last game in charge?
Huddersfield Town

Transfers I – Answers

1) Lauren arrived from which Spanish club in May 2000?
   Mallorca

2) Club stalwart Nigel Winterburn left Arsenal in the summer of 2000 to join which team?
   West Ham

3) Which midfielder was signed from Marseille in July 2000?
   Robert Pires

4) Which young English forward was bought from Everton in 2001?
   Francis Jeffers

5) Which two players left the club to join Barcelona in July 2000?
   Marc Overmars and Emmanuel Petit

6) From where did Arsenal sign Giovanni van Bronckhorst in 2001?
Rangers

7) Which future England international defender was sold to Birmingham in 2003?
Matthew Upson

8) Where did legendary goalkeeper David Seaman go after leaving Arsenal?
Manchester City

9) From which German club did Arsenal sign Jens Lehmann?
Borussia Dortmund

10) Robin van Persie was bought from which team in 2004?
Feyenoord

11) Which central midfielder was signed on a free from Marseille in July 2004?
Mathieu Flamini

12) Who did Martin Keown sign for after leaving Arsenal in 2004?
Leicester City

13) Which striker was bought from FC Copenhagen in 2005?
Nicklas Bendtner

14) Patrick Viera was sold to which Italian club in 2005?
Juventus

15) From which Premier League rival did Arsenal buy William Gallas in 2006?
Chelsea

16) Sol Campbell went to which team after being released in 2006?
Portsmouth

17) Which young midfielder was signed from Cardiff in the summer of 2008?
Aaron Ramsey

18) To which English club did Arsenal sell Freddie Ljungberg in 2007?

West Ham

19) Which Spanish club bought Aleksandr Hleb from Arsenal in 2008?

Barcelona

20) Which defender arrived from Ajax in July 2009?

Thomas Vermaelen

21) Which two players were sold to Manchester City in July 2009?

Emmanuel Adebayor and Kolo Toure

First Goals I – Answers

1) Robert Pires
   Lazio

2) Alexandre Lacazette
   Leicester City

3) Pierre-Emerick Aubameyang
   Everton

4) Sylvain Wiltord
   Coventry City

5) Robin Van Persie
   Manchester City

6) Gilberto Silva
   Liverpool

7) Jose Antonio Reyes
   Chelsea

8) Theo Walcott
   Chelsea

9) Ashley Cole
   Bradford City

10) Bacary Sagna
    Chelsea

11) Aaron Ramsey
    Fenerbahçe

12) Jack Wilshere
    Sheffield United

13) Samir Nasri
    West Brom

14) Andrey Arshavin
    Blackburn Rovers

Red Cards – Answers

1) Who was sent off on his Premier League debut against Newcastle in August 2011?
Gervinho

2) Alex Oxlade-Chamberlain handled the ball on the line versus Chelsea in 2014, but which player was incorrectly sent off instead?
Kieran Gibbs

3) Robin van Persie was given a second yellow card against Barcelona in March 2011 for what contentious reason?
Kicking the ball away

4) Ray Parlour was controversially sent off against which team in December 2001?
Newcastle

5) Sol Campbell was sent off for an alleged elbow on which Manchester United player in April 2003?
Ole Gunnar Solskjaer

6) Arsenal claimed a 1-1 draw with Middlesbrough despite being down to ten men after which defender saw red in February 2007?
Philippe Senderos

7) Patrick Vieira was sent off after a clash with which Leicester City player in August 2001?
Dennis Wise

8) Who was dismissed during the game with Southampton in April 2018?
Mohamed Elneny

9) Which player was dismissed in the 4-4 draw with Newcastle in 2011?
Abou Diaby

10) Laurent Koscielny was sent off early in the first half against which side during the last game of the 2017 season?
Everton

11) Which two Arsenal players were sent off versus Chelsea in September 2015?
Gabriel Paulista and Santi Cazorla

12) Arsenal claimed a 1-1 draw away to which side in the Champions League in November 2004 despite both Lauren and Patrick Vieira seeing red?
PSV Eindhoven

13) Which striker was sent off in the away fixture with Crystal Palace in January 2020?
Pierre-Emerick Aubameyang

14) Which defender was dismissed in the 2-2 draw with Chelsea in January 2020?
David Luiz

15) Wojciech Szczesny was sent off in the first half of a 2-0 loss to which club in the last 16 Champions League tie in February 2014?
Bayern Munich

Memorable Goals – Answers

1) Who did Thierry Henry score his final goal for Arsenal against?
   Sunderland

2) Thierry Henry returned to Arsenal in 2012 and scored on his second debut against which team in the FA Cup?
   Leeds United

3) How many times did Andrey Arshavin score against Liverpool in the April 2009 meeting between the two sides?
   4

4) Robert Pires produced a sublime lob against Aston Villa in 2002, which goalkeeper did he score past?
   Peter Schmeichel

5) Which player became Arsenal's youngest ever goal scorer by netting in the League Cup versus Wolves aged 16 years 6 months 28 days in December 2003?
Cesc Fabregas

6) Which team did Dennis Bergkamp score his final goal against in 2006?
West Brom

7) Bergkamp scored the Premier League goal of the season after produced a magnificent turn on which Newcastle defender in March 2002?
Nikos Dabizas

8) Thierry Henry scored his incredible solo goal against Spurs in November 2002 past which goalkeeper?
Kasey Keller

9) Which player scored the Premier League goal of the season for 2013/14 and 2014/15?
Jack Wilshere

10) Which full back won the goal of the month competition twice in the year 2000 for goals against Sheffield Wednesday and Chelsea?
Sylvinho

11) Patrick Vieira produced a wonderful chipped finish against which team in May 2005?
Everton

12) Aaron Ramsey scored the November 2013 goal of the month with his strike from the edge of the box versus which team?
Liverpool

13) Olivier Giroud scored with a spectacular scorpion flick against which team in January 2017?
Crystal Palace

14) Aaron Ramsey finished off a wonderful team goal away to which London club in October 2018?
Fulham

Memorable Games – Answers

1) Which former Arsenal player was sent off in the 5-2 win over Spurs in November 2012?
   Emmanuel Adebayor

2) Who scored a late brace as the Gunners won 5-2 against Tottenham in February 2012?
   Theo Walcott

3) Arsenal won the league at White Hart Lane in April 2004, what was the score that day?
   2-2

4) Arsenal threw away a four-goal lead to draw 4-4 with Newcastle in 2011, but which player had opened the scoring in the first minute?
   Theo Walcott

5) Arsenal were pegged back to a 4-4 draw with Spurs in October 2008 after which player scored an injury-time equaliser?
Aaron Lennon

6) Which two Arsenal players scored during their humiliating 8-2 defeat against Manchester United in 2011?
Theo Walcott and Robin van Persie

7) Who scored the final goal as Arsenal destroyed Middlesbrough 7-0 in January 2006?
Alexander Hleb

8) What was the final score as Arsenal tore Everton apart in May 2005?
7-0

9) Arsenal faced Chelsea in Arsene Wenger's 1000th game as manager, what was the score?
Chelsea 6-0 Arsenal

10) Arsenal beat Tottenham 5-4 away from home in November 2004, which Arsenal player scored from the penalty spot?
Lauren

11) Who did Arsenal beat 4-3 on the opening day of the 2017/18 Premier League season?
Leicester City

12) Who scored a hat-trick as Arsenal won 5-1 at West ham 5-1 in December 2016?
Alexis Sanchez

Transfers II – Answers

1) Arsenal signed which central midfielder from Everton in 2011?
   Mikel Arteta

2) From which German side did Arsenal sign Per Mertesacker?
   Werder Bremen

3) Olivier Giroud was bought from which French side in 2012?
   Montpellier

4) From which Spanish club did Arsenal buy Santi Cazorla in 2012?
   Malaga

5) Who returned to the club from AC Milan in 2013?
   Mathieu Flamini

6) Lukasz Fabianski signed for which team after leaving Arsenal in 2014?
   Swansea

7) Which Newcastle defender did Arsenal buy in 2014?
Mathieu Debuchy

8) Who did Arsenal buy from Borussia Mönchengladbach in 2016?
Granit Xhaka

9) Lukas Podolski was sold to who in 2015?
Galatasaray

10) From which English club was Rob Holding bought in 2016?
Bolton Wanderers

11) Shkodran Mustafi was bought from which Spanish club in 2016?
Valencia

12) Which attacking player was sold to Werder Bremen in August 2016?
Serge Gnabry

13) Alexandre Lacazette was bought from which team in 2017?
Lyon

14) Who did Arsenal buy from Bayer Leverkusen in June 2018?
Bernd Leno

15) Which defender was sold to West Brom in 2017?
Kieran Gibbs

16) Which midfielder was sold to Liverpool in August 2017?
Alex Oxlade-Chamberlain

17) Which experienced defender signed on a free from Juventus in 2018?
Stefan Lichtsteiner

18) Jack Wilshere left the club in 2018 to sign for which club on a free?
West Ham

19) Which attacker was bought from Lille in the summer of 2019?
Nicolas Pepe

20) Arsenal bought which defender from Celtic in 2019?
Kieran Tierney

21) Which attacker was sold to Everton in August 2019?
Alex Iwobi

Cup Games – Answers

1) How many FA Cup winner's medals did Aaron Ramsey collect during his time at Arsenal?
3

2) Arsenal beat Southampton 1-0 in the 2003 FA Cup final, who scored the winner?
Robert Pires

3) Arsenal beat Hull City 3-2 after extra time in the 2014 FA Cup final, who scored the equaliser in normal time for the Gunners?
Laurent Koscielny

4) Arsenal beat Liverpool 6-3 away from home in the League Cup Quarter Final of 2007, who scored four times for the Gunners?
Julio Baptista

5) Who scored the opening goal in the 2017 FA Cup final win over Chelsea?
Alexis Sanchez

6) Which team did Arsenal beat 4-0 in the 2015 FA Cup final?
Aston Villa

7) Who scored the decisive spot kick as Arsenal beat Manchester United on penalties in the 2005 FA Cup final?
Patrick Vieira

8) Nottingham Forest knocked Arsenal out of the FA Cup at the 3rd round stage in 2018 by what score-line?
4-2

9) Who scored the last-minute winner for Birmingham to clinch the League Cup in 2011?
Obafemi Martins

10) Arsenal lost to Middlesbrough in the 2004 League Cup Semi Final, who was in goal for Arsenal in the 2nd leg?
Graham Stack

11) Who scored twice for Chelsea as they defeated Arsenal 2-1 in the 2007 League Cup Final?
Didier Drogba

12) Liverpool and Arsenal played out an unbelievable tie in the League Cup in October 2019, what was the score in normal time before Liverpool won on penalties?
5-5

First Goals II – Answers

1) Sol Campbell
   Chelsea

2) Cesc Fàbregas
   Wolverhampton Wanderers

3) Alex Oxlade-Chamberlain
   Shrewsbury Town

4) Per Mertesacker
   Tottenham Hotspur

5) Lukas Podolski
   Liverpool

6) Olivier Giroud
   Coventry City

7) Santi Cazorla
   Liverpool

8) Nicklas Bendtner
   Newcastle United

9) Hector Bellerín
   Aston Villa

10) Alexis Sanchez
    Beşiktaş

11) Mesut Özil
    Napoli

12) Danny Welbeck
    Tottenham Hotspur

13) Granit Xhaka
    Hull City

14) Nicolas Pepe
    Aston Villa

European Games – Answers

1) Thierry Henry scored a stunning solo goal against Real Madrid in 2006, which goalkeeper did he score past?
   Iker Casillas

2) Arsenal recorded a famous away win by demolishing Inter Milan in the Champions League in November 2003, what was the final score?
   Inter Milan 1-5 Arsenal

3) Who scored the late winner as Chelsea knocked Arsenal out of the Champions League at the Quarter Final stage in 2004?
   Wayne Bridge

4) Who scored the only goal of the tie as Arsenal reached the 2006 Champions League Final by beating Villarreal on aggregate?
   Kolo Toure

5) Jens Lehmann made a vital, late penalty save from which player to prevent that 2006 Semi Final from going to extra time?
Juan Roman Riquelme

6) Who scored the opening goal in the 2006 Champions League Final?
Sol Campbell

7) Which English team knocked Arsenal out of the 2008 Champions League in the Quarter Finals?
Liverpool

8) Which team knocked Arsenal out of the Champions League at the last 16 stage in both 2013 and 2014?
Bayern Munich

9) Which side did Arsenal knock out of Champions League in the qualifying round in 2009?
Celtic

10) Arsenal lost to Atletico Madrid in the 2018 Europa League Semi Final, who scored the only goal in the 1-0 defeat in the 2nd leg?
Diego Costa

11) Who scored the Arsenal goal as they lost 4-1 in the 2019 Europa League Final against Chelsea?
Alex Iwobi

12) Arsenal lost the 2000 UEFA Cup Final 4-1 on penalties to which team?
Galatasary

13) Who scored the late winner as Arsenal beat Barcelona 2-1 in the 1st leg of their Champions League knockout tie in 2011?
Andrey Arshavin

14) Which team did Arsenal beat 7-0 in the Champions League in October 2007?
Slavia Prague

Printed in Great Britain
by Amazon

54401695R00036